CAMOUFLAGED NIGHTMARES: A MEMOIR OF THE VIETNAM WAR

by

Jake Seveneau

SEVENEAU

The contents of this work, including, but not limited to, the accuracy of events, people, and places depicted; opinions expressed; permission to use previously published materials included; and any advice given or actions advocated are solely the responsibility of the author, who assumes all liability for said work and indemnifies the publisher against any claims stemming from publication of the work.

All Rights Reserved
Copyright © 2023 by Jake Seveneau

No part of this book may be reproduced or transmitted, downloaded, distributed, reverse engineered, or stored in or introduced into any information storage and retrieval system, in any form or by any means, including photocopying and recording, whether electronic or mechanical, now known or hereinafter invented without permission in writing from the publisher.

Dorrance Publishing Co
585 Alpha Drive
Suite 103
Pittsburgh, PA 15238
Visit our website at *www.dorrancebookstore.com*

ISBN: 979-8-8860-4137-8
eISBN: 979-8-8860-4802-5

Table of Contents

Part 1 – Before   1

01 Journal Entry 29 January 1969
   – Old House   2
02 Clouds Form in the Eastern Sky   10
03 In Query of Rhyme and Reason   12
04 Hoops   13
05 The American Dream   14
06 December Mourning   16

Part 2 – During   21

07 Welcome Mat   23
08 Journal Entry 7 May 1971
   – Assessment of the Situation   24
09 So I Was Told   27
10 Love Your Neighbour as Yourself   29
11 Letter #1 – Old House Crew
   – Preliminary Letter   32
12 Letter #2 – Old House Crew
   – Group Letter   34
13 Letter #3 – Leo and Kathleen   58
14 Letter #4 – Bob and Susan   65
15 Letter #5 – Patrick
   and Michelle w/Limerick   69
16 Letter #6 – To Marti   75
17 Poem – Mariah   81
18 Camouflaged Nightmares   82

19	Journal Entry 28 August 1971 – CRB Ammo Dump	87
20	Sandpiper	91
21	Journal Entry 18 October 1971 – MEDCAP	92
22	War is About Children	96
23	Journal Entry 10 December 1971 – It was the Little Things	99
24	Toy Soldiers	104
25	Evil Fog	105
26	Infinite Burdens	106
27	Women Too	109
28	Row After Row	112
29	Enemies	113
30	Midnight Mercy Plane	115
31	Merry Christmas 1971	117
32	Black Marshmallow Dimension	119
33	Journal Entry 29 February 1972 – Tan Son Nhut to Travisty	122

Part 3 – After — **125**

34	Journal Entry – The Ides of March	126
35	Difficult Choices	129
36	Random Patterns	132
37	All in My Head	133
38	Bad Days – Good Days	136
39	The Second War	139
40	The Cure	140
41	War and Peace	141
42	Shrink Wrapped Sessions	142

43	All I Can Do	143
44	To Be Healed	145
45	Total and Permanent	146
46	Note to Self	148
47	Saigon Has Fallen – 30 April 1975	150
48	Last Will and Testimony	151
49	Postscript – The Result	154

Illustrations

01. Old House   ix
02. December Mourning   19
03. Phase I Medical   22
04. If God Is Love   31
05. Peace Begins Within   31
06. Truth Must Be Sought   65
07. My Father's House   74
08. Love   75
09. Mariah   80
10. Camouflaged Nightmares   86
11. War Is About Children   98
12. Infinite Burdens   108
13. Black Marshmallow Dimension   121
14. All in My Head   135
15. Bad Days/Good Days   138
16. Old Man   155

Dedications

This work is dedicated to the following:

YHWH (God) who saves souls according to His Word, by granting us the grace to have faith in Yeshua Ha'Maschiyach (Jesus the Messiah) and His teachings;

All of the children for all of the joy, love, and faith they bring, helping us to understand and accept God's will;

All those who were minding their own business and working to survive when war crept up and struck them down, killing many and disabling multitudes more;

Those who work to preserve lives rather than taking them;

Those who yet suffer from war's after-effects and have learned enough to sincerely preach peace and love and strive to attain these things from the teachings of Yeshua Ha'Maschiyach;

The multitude of true disciples of Yeshua who have prayed for and with me in seeking to understand, possess, and communicate truth and faith in Yeshua;

All of the travelers who rendered various forms of assistance to me as I have wandered the globe seeking truth and striving to fulfill my God-given purpose;

The many caring souls who inspired, encouraged, and assisted me in editing, publishing, and distributing this work;

And to all of the cooks and waitresses who have allowed me to sit for hours on end while soaking up coffee and refining this book.

Abbreviations

ARVN: Army of the Republic of Vietnam
ASAP: As Soon As Possible
CO: Conscientious Objector
CRB: Cam Ranh Bay
DSM: Diagnostic and Statistical Manual of Mental Disorders
EM Club: Enlisted Men''s Club
EOD: Explosives Ordinance and Demolition
GI: Government Issue
JAG: Judge Advocate General
MEDCAP: Medical Civilian Action Program
NCOIC: Non-Commissioned Officer in Charge
NVA: North Vietnamese Army
OH: Old House (a communal house for college students)
OIC: Officer in Charge
PDR: Physicians' Desk Reference
PO: Post Office
ROK: Republic of Korea
Roost: Attic apartment at Old House
R&R: Rest and Relaxation
RVN: Republic of Vietnam
RVNAF: Republic of Viet Nam Air Force
SAT: Security Assistance Team
SSB: Single Side Band Radio

SMSgt. Senior Master Sergeant
SSgt: Staff Sergeant
STAT: abbreviation for "statim," meaning "immediately"
TDY: Temporary Duty
UCMJ: Uniform Code of Military Justice
VC: Viet Cong

PART 1
BEFORE

01. Journal Entry - 29 January 1969
Old House

Coming home from work this evening I found that the postman had left me a formal invitation to my currently worst nightmare: military conscription.

If only I had not been so stubborn about wanting to officially declare my core reason for being opposed to the war and had not taken the summer off, I could have qualified for a Student Deferment, but instead, as this journal testifies to, I foolishly insisted on going the strict CO pathway, which I now regret.

Oh why, oh why did I not listen to Leo and the others?

In the end what difference does it make that I stood up to the system and went through all sorts of crap simply to register my beliefs concerning hatred and violence?

Just as was predicted by so many, all of our efforts, including Judge Leo's excellent presentation of my case to obtain a Conscientious Objector Deferment, have been in vain and my application has been denied on the basis of two pieces of evidence.

First of all I have only been a Christian for a short time and do not belong to a church that historically teaches nonviolence, which is a major mark against me.

Second, I was photographed at that antiwar rally pushing the cop who had just hit Michelle with his baton and as a result I was charged with assaulting an officer and resisting arrest.

That was most damaging to my case, in spite of other incidents where I have stood firm when confronted by violence that I have not always acted peacefully in the presence of aggression.

And if not for the fact that the cop had broken Michelle's arm and that Leo brought that to light in my defence, I would not have been released and probably would have done six months.

Anyway, the resulting situation is that I have officially lost my final appeal and am being ordered to report to Fort Fiasco Induction Centre late next month for an examination to see if I am physically and mentally fit for military duty, an examination which I will undoubtedly pass.

In other words, I am faced with just three, equally difficult to swallow, options.

The first of these is to abscond to a neutral country, such as Canada or Sweden, and beg for asylum.

The second option is to officially refuse induction and face the consequences.

The third is to volunteer for the military and serve as some type of medic or medical technician. Of course, since my final appeal I have spent a serious amount of time considering each of these options and this is where my head is currently at concerning them.

Option One: leaving this country in protest of the war is not a position I can see myself taking for a few of reasons.

First of all I am fairly certain the government will never allow draft dodgers to simply return to the US unimpaired once the war is over even once we are proven right.

Second, I very much like living and going to school here at least as much if not more than as I detest those things that are wrong with this country.

Third, there is my developing relationship with Marti, Leo, and Kathleen, whom I now count as family and do not want to leave behind.

Option Two: refusing to be inducted into the military is no good both because it leads to a minimum of two years in prison and I am convinced that I would not survive such a violent and insane place.

Option Three: volunteering to serve as a medic is somewhat of a possibility because, if I understand that path according to the veterans and recruiters I have spoken to, the military gives volunteers a series of aptitude tests and allows them to select two or three advanced training schools they would like to attend.

Then, if one has an applicable background, knowledge and can pass the entrance exams, they are all but guaranteed to attend one of those schools and when they graduate to serve in that capacity.

Well, having passed all of my science courses, advanced first aid and senior life saving and having worked part time as a nurse's assistant for nearly six months now, I am pretty sure that I can pass the tests required to become some sort of medical technician.

Especially if I intentionally get a number of questions for other fields of study wrong and score as high as possible in the medical and science fields.

But then, what about the war?

Which branch of the military am I best suited for, and which one will allow me to avoid being pushed into the combat debacle, as much as possible?

Being a Christian and a CO, it is rather difficult to see myself in any branch of the military, but it seems I am being forced to choose one, and so I want to consider them all and analyze each one's general conditions before making that choice.

There are the Marines, Army, Navy, Coast Guard, and Air Force.

As for the Marines and having had an ex-Marine and Korean War veteran as a custodian for more than three years, I definitely do not want to go in that direction because I believe they are far too brainwashed, violent, and always in the forward ranks of whatever armed conflict is occurring at any given time.

Therefore, scratch the Marines.

Then there is the Army, which I understand one can volunteer for and serve just eighteen months as opposed to doing a two- or four-year hitch, but then I also hear that almost all draftees and short-term volunteers end up doing a tour in some combat unit in Vietnam.

In other words, Army grunts, similar to the Marines, often serve in combat zones, so no thank you to that choice as well.

As for the Navy and Coast Guard, I see more negative points than positive in both water-based services, where I am concerned.

To begin with, I cannot stand being in small, enclosed spaces and get radically ill when on a boat, whether large or small if the water is at all rough.

Plus, there is the fact that some Navy medics get assigned to Marine combat units, which amounts to being in the Marines.

Also, I am aware of the fact there are several Coast Guard river patrol boats assigned to Vietnam, which is not my idea of high-quality time.

So, thank you but no thanks to either of those options.

Then finally there is the Air Force, which I am definitely not attracted to as they also shoot and bomb people, many of whom are reported to be innocent civilians.

And yet Air Force medical personnel rarely, if ever, serve in combat units, and I am fairly

Jake Seveneau

certain their bases are more to the rear in war zones, which is a good thing, especially if one ends up being assigned to Vietnam.

Also, it is my understanding if one volunteers for the Air Force, it is for a full four years and yet there is the distinct possibility someone with my sort of knowledge and experience getting into a fairly decent medical tech school, which would be a good thing as I would like to become a laboratory technician so that I can work to help save lives rather than take them.

That and there is the point that such courses of study can easily take up to as much as the first two years of one's enlistment, leaving just two years or a bit more to serve in the field.

Anyway, as far as I can see, if I absolutely must serve time in the military, it might as well be in the Air Force where I have a good chance of avoiding combat and getting a decent education in the process.

And that would amount to education and practice which can lead to some college credits or even translate to a decent civilian job when one is finally discharged.

Well, it is now nearly midnight and I need to get some sleep, so I will close this entry and "hit the rack," as my former ex-marine guardian would say.

Then tomorrow morning I will discuss these thoughts with Leo, Kathleen, and Marti to get their opinions, but for now I will just pray about and then sleep on it.

02. Clouds Form in the Eastern Sky

Clouds form in the eastern sky
causing me to wonder why
do they want to hide the moon and stars

Is it a symbol of the times
Is there prophecy in that long grey line
or is this just the way that some clouds are

I search myself and others for some answer
hoping we'll be offered some relief
but the wind arises like some desperate dancer
and the coming storm will test all our beliefs

The clouds continue on their way
moving closer every day
the lightning and the thunder roar like canon

And from the boiling stratosphere
comes burning rain, chaos, and fear
and other things that hell must have a hand in

So I strain my mind but still there is no answer
no hint we might be offered some relief
The only thing we have left now is hope
as the storm assails our most sincere beliefs

And it soon becomes hurricane
destroying every weathervane
so no one knows which way it will blow next

All we can do is to hang on
pray we'll see another dawn
and that the wind will not come back from the west

So I kneel and pray but there is still no answer
no hint we might be offered some relief
The only thing we have left now is hope
as the storm devours all of our beliefs

03. In Query of Rhyme and Reason

what is right
is there light

can truth ever be revealed
has it ever been concealed

capitol domes
old gravestones

ivory towers and ancient mores
laws of the land and keeping score

ethics and morality
reasoning and reality

considering ongoing events
who is able to pay such rent

questions asked
present and past

heirs of responsibility
is anyone ever truly free

04. Hoops

You know the hoops we all jump through
day after day after day
I speculate there is just one place
where all those hoops are made

Hoops of red and probably green
maybe yellow or orange or blue
Hoops of paperwork and money
Hoops of things to prove

I propose they are all made in the bowels of hell
in a demon-staffed factory
Bureaucratic hoops and lovers' hoops
and hoops of legalese

And as we do our daily dances
thinking it all necessary
little demons are improving these hoops
to make them ever more scary

and at every one of their break times
they watch us doing hoop tricks
as they sip tea and coffee
and laugh themselves quite sick

05. American Dream

The American Dream sweet American Dream
infiltrating the world and so it must be

as nations are conquered by whatever means
bullets or stock shares you hear Wall Street scream

the American Dream sweet American Dream
surrender to it and accept its grandiose scheme

We will send diplomats and send the Marines
send entrepreneurs with mammoth machines

You will eat McDonald's and build big shopping malls
profess to your people they can have it all

the drive to succeed gaining money and fame
prestige and power while ignoring all shame

and we will all profit when you swallow the bait
then maybe you will see it but oops it is too late

The American Dream sweet American Dream
infecting mankind with ludicrous schemes

the American Dream mad American theme
can any escape its cold rule supreme

this is problem also the question
but what is the answer to power's obsession

the American Dream sweet American Dream
surrender to it accept its grand scheme

06. December Mourning

On a hot December morning
they carried young Davis away
on a pallet of wood and canvas
on that first of many sad days

An explosion had shattered the evening before
a bullet interrupted his thoughts
At twenty-five his enlistment ended
but there was still more to be taught

As the freedom bird carried him upward
above the jungle toward his childhood home
a revelation opened wide
He would not leave that place alone

Tens of thousands would follow
as the reaper seized the reins
and insanely swinging his razor scythe
destroyed leagues of grain

until rivers turned to crimson
and peace could not be defined
through the ever-rising ash heaps
which buried every logical line

Yet as that image bore its misery
his soul drifted off to sleep
beyond the endless fog of war
far above the turquoise sea

It was a cold December afternoon
they carried his body away
in a casket covered by an American Flag
as the congregation prayed

In a mournful ceremony
near his childhood home
on a hill of cold hard earth
amid rows of silent stones

His former masters gave his wife the flag
and a medal to put on display
But "Thank you, sorry, he served us well"
was all that they could say

For no one could ever bring him back
no matter how hard they tried
Nor silence the lies that lured him
into the ambush where he died

Thus sorrow echoes through the hills
around his family's front door
saying to all who are willing to hear
"This is the sole reward of war."

While back in the jungle where he had worked
his revelation is bequeathed

as dragons spew out orange rain
as extreme prejudice is unleashed

that tens of thousands will follow him
just as his dreams foretold
carrying signs that simply read
"for sale are our souls"

December Mourning

PART 2
During

Phase 1 Medical

07. Welcome Mat

On the front step of the hooch
a rubber mat bears the standard greeting
WELCOME
as if the present tenants were truly glad to see me

Staring at it I contemplate
does hell not have
the same sort of mat
at its gate

08. Journal Entry - 7 May 1971
CRB RVN

Having been here long enough now, I have rotated through every section of the lab and am now assigned to haematology, which just happens to be my favourite section.

In fact, I have started to classify and collect slides showing various types of malaria, also some showing sickle cell enema and leukemia, as I hope someday to write papers about each

Anyway, I have had the time to get to know my hooch-mates, coworkers and some other people, such as a few nurses and a couple of doctors.

And throughout this introductory process I have begun to understand, to some degree, that like anywhere on earth the people here are just like my high school friend, Bernie, used to describe them.

So here I paraphrase his analysis of the human condition.

There are just three kinds of people in the world: men, women and jerks.

The main goal in life is to stay out of the third category as much as possible, while openly admitting that we all stumble into it every once in a while and should repent whenever that happens.

Unfortunately, the sad truth is that there are some people who live their entire lives in that third category, believing all the while that they are superior to most others and right to do so.

------------ ~~~~~~~~~~~ ------------

Then too, at this time I wish to make a note here about discovering that even among the lifers not all of them dislike me or feel that I am wrong and should be punished for being what many call a "conch" (Conscientious Objector).

In fact, even the NCOIC of the lab here has encouraged me to stick to my beliefs when it comes to the war and civil rights movement, but just not to be on anybody's case about these things, unless they truly need to be put in their place like SMSgt Butthead, my former boss at Riverside.

After all, I know per fact that he psychologically abused his own daughter, sent me here simply for being a CO, and sent another man here just because he is in an interracial marriage.

In other words, the man is definitely a lifelong jerk and needs someone to help him extract his head from the place it is stuck in.

And yes, I am fully aware of the fact it is not my place to pass judgment on him, as only God can pass judgment on any of us; however, I am supposed to be discerning and therefore cannot help but honestly assess the situation.

Amen and goodnight.

09. So I Was Told

Throughout my schooling I was told
ours is a Christian nation
founded by Christian people
with a constitution and Bill of Rights
based on Christian principles…
so I was told

We recited a pledge of allegiance every day
which clearly states we are "One Nation Under God"
and our money has "In God We Trust" engraved on it
which supposedly means the God of the Bible
the Father who Jesus spoke about…
so I was told

Back then "God 'n' country" was all one word
Back then the trinity was red, white and blue
which made Matthew, Mark, Luke and John
all patriots
enterprising capitalists…
so I was lead to believe

Furthermore, I was told
it is the duty of every citizen
to believe in the United States of America
to obey its laws
support its wars

hate its enemies and
kill them
as that this is courage and righteousness…
so I was told

Then I grew up and was sent here to war
where all I had been told was tested

"You have heard that it was said, 'You shall love your neighbour and hate your enemy. But I say to you, love your enemies, bless those who curse you, do good to those who hate you, and pray for those who spitefully use you and persecute you, that you may be sons of your Father in heaven.'" Matthew 5:4345a NKJV

10. Love Your Neighbour As Yourself

If I say that "God is Love"
what does that mean
unless I truly love my neighbours
　love myself
　my enemies

In God's Word
that is the second great commandment

Feed the hungry
with food for the body
　the mind
　and soul

Clothe and shelter the poor
with garments and houses for the body
　the mind
　and soul
Care about their present
　their past
　and future

Old wounds yet open cannot be ignored
Wounds not fully healed may yet be infected

Jake Seveneau

We lack not in agencies
not in time
but in plans
  volunteers
  supplies

We lack for love
  lack for truth
  for understanding
  repentance
  forgiveness

We must seek these things and deal in them
seek God
and follow His instructions

If God is Love

Peace Begins Within

11. Letter #1 - Day 317 - CRB-RVN

Dear Old House Crew,

It is late Thursday afternoon here and I have just returned from an eleven-day TDY assignment, during which I had no access to mail either coming or going.

Thus, finding your packet of letters waiting here is a somewhat serendipitous thing and I thank all of you deeply for it.

Anyway, as soon as I get back to my hooch I will begin to read them and make notes pertaining to the most common comments and questions, which I will deal with in one letter to all of you.

That way you can get together and have one person read it to all involved, or else pass it around until all have read it.

Following that initial letter I will compose and post a separate letter to each person or couple in reply to your more personal comments and questions.

Finally, I want you all to know I am doing as well as can be expected under the circumstances and that I continue to pray for each and every one of you, as well as for myself, to have complete faith in the Lord, to be delivered from this madness we all live in.

Please pray for the same and ask Sue to play "Put Your Hand in the Hand of the Man" during her next shift at the radio station.

Sincerely,

Jake

12. Letter #2 - Day 318 - CRB-RVN

Dear Old House Crew,

As stated in the brief letter posted yesterday, after reading all of your letters through twice I drew up a list of your common comments and questions and shall be dealing with all of those in this letter.

Then, after this letter is complete, I will deal with your personal questions and comments in separate letters addressed directly to those who presented them, not to create any soap opera scenarios but for privacy's sake.

Now, to begin with, all of you asked me to be more open about what is happening with me and so I will deal with that request first.
You say that it is obvious that something is going on with me beyond what I have been willing to share, but that I am so stingy with information you cannot determine just what it is, be it physical, spiritual, and/or psychological.

All right, in responding to these questions and comments I will be as open far enough for you to know what the basic situation is, but that is as deep as I will go for now.

Why? Because this is not a movie or a "just war" such as Aristotle, Plato, Augustine, or Aquinas wrote about.

As you know, I do not believe there is, or ever has been, any such thing.

Here, as in all wars, there are no good guys and no satisfactory conclusions to be drawn, only senselessness, frustration, and endless tears to be shed.

In fact, it is all far beyond what any sane person should be able to imagine, let alone have to deal with and because I love all of you, I do not wish to infect you with the full load of the political and militaristic feces that this situation is composed of.

Thus, I will describe the situation in general terms, hoping that you may cease to worry about me personally and can spend more time thinking about positive things, such as continuing to demonstrate against all wars and for civil rights to be firmly established for everyone on earth, if either of those outcomes is possible.

To begin with I will tell you quite honestly that I am in satisfactory physical shape and have no complaints in that area.

Spiritually speaking, things are relatively steady, and I still read the Bible and pray pretty much every day.

However, I confess to not reading the scriptures every single day nor praying in a formal manner; therefore, I can use all of the intercessory prayer and encouragement you can muster.

Then there is my psychological state, wherein a few things definitely need some straightening out and, yes, I have talked to a couple of doctors about these matters.

The first was a physician at Phan Rang who saw me just before I finished my TDY assignment there.

At the time I was suffering from insomnia and having some pretty severe anxiety attacks.

He prescribed some pills to treat the symptoms, then suggested I see the local shrink and be thoroughly tested upon returning here to CRB, which is what has been and will be happening early next week.

Anyway, the doctor at PR put a note in my file suggesting that I may be suffering from what used to be called "shell shock" as a result of various incidents that have occurred here.

Then the shrink here at CRB said that condition is now known as "combat fatigue" and he put some notes in my medical records concerning it.

But due to our busy schedules I have not been fully tested as yet, although, as stated, that will begin happening this coming Tuesday.

As for one of the incidents just mentioned which occurred the day after the VC hit the ammo dump here at CRB late last August.

At the time, I was riding on a SAT jeep, and while standing by, waiting for EOD to clear a path for us, an unexpected blast knocked me backwards into a jeep and as a result I was unconscious for a minute or so.

After that the NCOIC I was riding with (SSgt. Townes) took me to the ER to be examined despite my being able to stand up and feeling relatively well, except for a slight headache and a bit of dizziness.

The doctor who examined me ordered X-rays of my head and neck, then concluded I had a slight concussion but was probably all right and should not suffer any lasting effects.

However, throughout September-October and especially during my TDY to Phan Rang in November-December, I had increasingly noticeable problems, which I have tracked and which the doctor at Phan Rang noted and gave me some prescriptions for.

Then, too, last week while in Nha Trang, I had a very lucid flashback while performing a somewhat complicated chemistry test so I had to repeat the entire test because I could not swear to having performed it strictly according to the instructions the first time through.

That was when I realized something has to be done about the entire situation, primarily for the sake of the patients who rely upon my accuracy to stay alive and well.

After all, if I screw up a test the doctor's diagnosis might be wrong and that could jeopardize the patient's well-being, which would *not* help in fulfilling the Hippocratic Oath which I strive to follow, even though I am not a physician.

In any case, instead of praying and reading the Word every day, I have been slowly and steadily sinking into what I call the "Black Marshmallow Dimension," which is not a good place to be.

In fact, at times it feels like the war is gradually swallowing me.

To be perfectly honest, I do not feel that anything is going to change this condition, save getting out of here as soon as possible.

Still, I must try and do all that I can to affect all of the changes required to bring me back around to normal, so that I can do my job to the best of my ability for the sake of all concerned.

So that is what I seek to accomplish and ask you to pray for.

However, as far as seeing a chaplain or JAG officer about applying for an early discharge of some sort, as Leo has suggested, I have not spoken to either one.

This is primarily because the ones I know are extremely patriotic and they do not like being told how the US was *not* founded by devout Christians but by a bunch of capitalistic misogynistic Masons and their buddies, in my humble opinion.

They were all white men who voted to wage war against their king, to legalize slavery and commit genocide concerning the original inhabitants of the land.

They believed in the populist teachings of Manifest Destiny and the superiority of white males over all other human beings and of course, you know where I stand on such teachings.

Anyway, I have no common ground with those who hold to such teachings, which would be necessary to have a logical conversation concerning my situation, and thus I see no reason to consult with them.

However, the fact that two doctors have already written in my medical records that my deteriorating psychological condition is due to my experiences here should be sufficient to apply for a medical discharge whenever I finally return to the States.

And if the shrinks back home confirm this diagnosis, the military establishment should have no choice but to discharge me as soon as possible.

However, I will simply bide my time, follow the shrink's instructions, and wait until I am back in the States where things should be less confusing.

Once there, hopefully my new OIC will see the logic in handing me a medical discharge, as that seems like the best and most logical solution to this mess.

So that is the overview of my current condition and I hope it does not bum you out too much.

But for now, let us move on to a far more positive subject.

------------ ~~~~~~~~~~~ ------------

All of you reported that Marti has already successfully defended her thesis and thus has completed all requirements for her PhD.

Plus you mentioned that the paper will be published in the fall edition of the *Math and Science Review*, which I agree is impressive.

Also a few of you asked how I feel about her brilliant success and note that she hopes I will be home in time to attend her graduation ceremony.

Well, knowing Marti, none of this surprises me and actually, I am amazed it did not happen sooner.

But as for the timing of the ceremony, my tour is supposed to end in mid-April, and if that is the case, then the opportunity for leave might be in sync with the chosen date for the grad ceremony.

However, if I am sent back to the States early but not discharged at that time, I would probably miss the big event simply because that is when a huge number of people want to take leave and most of them apply for it up to a year in advance, which makes it almost impossible for latecomers to obtain leave at that time.

In other words, at this point my being home for the ceremony appears to be a fifty-fifty shot that depends on what the doctors determine concerning my condition and whether it is deserving of early rotation and perhaps a medical discharge.

For as we all know military commanders and chiefs do not consider themselves obligated to adhere to any sort of legal system, including the UCMJ or Constitution.

In general, they do not see soldiers as citizens, rather as government property, and they do not actually care about looking at verifiable evidence or holding fair hearings when it comes to their situations.

Instead, their primary objective, as with most politicians, is to obtain and maintain control of their positions of power.

Meaning they can keep me on active duty for up to six years, no questions asked, no leave allowed, if that is what they decide is best for them.

Besides that, if I have committed any infractions (according to their definition of the word), they can retain and jail me for as long as they like and no one can stop them.

However, if they determine it would be better for them to ship me back to the States early and hand me an immediate medical discharge, which is what I hope and pray will happen, then please be assured that I will be home at the appointed time.

Now, as for my contribution to the big celebration, regardless of whether or not I am present, I have been saving a bit of money each month to pay for a small gift for each of the three graduates.

Then too I will be sending Patrick a check to cover a few rolls of film for photos, especially of Marti, Sue, and Bob all wearing their caps and gowns and holding their sheepskins out for the camera, as a testimony to their friendship, brilliance and good looks.

Also, I will send Papa Olson a check to pay for a seriously bourgeoisie smorgasbord to include the original OH crew (except for James, of course) and their parents and siblings.

Thus, whether or not I am able to attend, I pray it all goes very well and that all of you have a splendid time.

------------ ~~~~~~~~~~~~ ------------

Break for evening chow.

------------ ~~~~~~~~~~~~ ------------

Now about the recent demonstrations you have all been involved in:

The packet about these activities included Bob's articles from the *Herald* and *Back Alley*, Sue's detailed descriptions and Patrick's photos of the teach-in and candlelight peace walk from Mount Olive to the university chapel were all very encouraging.

I really poured over all that material and can see the direct involvement of the entire crew and certain family members in organising and putting on the events.

And of course, it causes me to wish I could have been there with you instead of being here merely reading about these things after the fact.

First of all, the teach-in sounds quite well organized, and primarily focused on the history of colonialism and the wars in Southeast Asia over the past two centuries, as compared to the same time frame in America.

These are things that everyone should be aware of.

Such an excellent idea and I highly suspect that Ms. History Buff Susan directed its planning and execution.

Also, considering how she usually gets in front of a large audience, I am quite impressed that she delivered the actual lecture.

Second, I am very glad to learn that the candlelight peace walk was in fact quite peaceful and that no one hassled anyone else during it, as at some such events we hear about where counter-protesters come out and everyone wastes their energy just screaming back and forth at each other.

Furthermore, I can see how the entire crew probably helped to plan and execute that event and I hope people simply walked and prayed for everyone involved in this mess, that we may all come to see the truth.

Actually, in my humble opinion, both events are huge accomplishments, especially the prayers for our opponents and their loved ones.

After all, how can we effectively demonstrate and teach peace and understanding unless we are peaceful and willing to listen to our opponents' viewpoints and desires?

In fact, if I read the Bible correctly, we are all supposed to pray for our enemies and political higher-ups on all sides of the issues, that we will all see the light and come together to do God's will and not our own.

Anyway, my deepest thanks to everyone who participated in those events, and I thank Marti for carrying the plaque with my name on it, plus I pray that your voices were heard and listened to by those in power.

------------ ~~~~~~~~~~~ ------------

Now, if I understand things correctly concerning everyone's plans for the farmstead and such, and please tell me if I do not, the first new resident there will be our fearless leader, Judge Leo Rosenbaum, as he is adjusting his initial plan to retire from the bench at the end of next year and instead will retire in early May, then immediately move out to the farmstead where he will live in the new trailer with Otis while overseeing the remodelling and expansion of the house and workshop?

You also say that Kathleen has adjusted her plans to move to the farmstead at the same time and, instead of retiring in June, will remain at Mount Olive through the summer, then officially retire on September first, when she will join Leo at the farmstead once the house remodelling project is complete.

Is all of that correct so far?

Anyway, then in mid-September a portable classroom is be set up, and starting in early October,

Kathleen will begin offering basic and mid-level classes in subjects such as reading, writing, basic math and personal bookkeeping, to anyone in the immediate area who needs help with such things and is willing to work for it

But why has no mention been made of the things that were being discussed this past year, such as developing the south side of the lake and working in league with the Ojibwa people who own properties along the north shore?

Furthermore, have you given up on the ideas we discussed before the farmstead was purchased?

- Reviewing the book *Five Acres and Independence* by M.G. Kains
- Cutting back on public access to the lake
- Establishing firm limits on fishing and hunting by anyone, including those whose property borders the lake
- Re-establishing native species of fauna and flora
- Classes in cyclical farming and basic construction methods
- Establishing a book and organic food market by the highway
- Constructing a sugar-bushing station at the west end of the lake

Please let me know where you are presently at with these ideas.

Then, too, in relation to these things, there are a few questions here about what I might do after being discharged, and the top three guesses are
1. Return to school and continue living at Old House
2. Live and work at the farmstead
3. Find a job, perhaps as a lab tech, and live in my own place

Well, all things considered, I am nowhere close to making any firm decisions concerning the future, except that I will probably continue school but change my area of study from science and medicine to focus on literature and theology.

That and I would like to continue living, in the Roost, at Old House at least for a while.

We shall see.

Anyway, moving right along...

In Sue's letter, she stated she was just over one month pregnant and that she and Bob have moved into the guest cottage at her parents' house, where they can start saving money while Bob completes his master's in journalism and Sue establishes herself as a personal tutor and editor.

So, congratulations to the happy couple, the grandparents, in-laws, outlaws and especially to the first member of the next generation of the Old

House Crew, plus everyone else connected to them.

Then, too, I see Bob has continued working part-time at the *Back Alley* until he completes his degree and has moved up from being an occasional contributor to a monthly columnist at the *Herald*, which I assume is a reasonably well-paid position.

Also, he states that his present goal is to write one piece per month about the war for the *Back Alley*, and one about the civil rights movement for the *Herald*, which sounds like a good thing to do.

Furthermore, he asks if I am still keeping a journal and, if so, am I willing to share some of the entries with him for his anti-war column.

Plus, both he and Sue ask if I have considered publishing some of my poetry and/or some short stories together as a mixed collection, and whether I would consider having Sue help me with such a project.

In response to the first question, I agree that there is far too little accurate information being published about both the war and the civil rights movement, and it is good to know that someone is trying to rectify that situation.
However, for the same reasons given in the beginning of this letter, I am reluctant to get involved and do not want to be quoted or published

in any form, for any reason, while still in the military as it could easily affect my present situation in a negative manner.

Even if one simply said, "I know someone who is involved in the war and they said this or that," it is too close to home as it might be traced back to me and cause problems which I do not need.

So please keep the things I write and draw to yourselves.

Day 319 - CRB-RVN

As for Michelle and Patrick, my understanding is that she is scheduled to finish her studies in registered nursing in late August, and upon completion has been promised a position at University Hospital, where Patrick is to begin his internship in September.
How serendipitous!

Also I see that they are communicating with a couple of different missions groups, one in South Africa and one in Central America, concerning a possible short-term mission trip for the winter of '72-'73.

Meaning they have not yet made a firm decision about which path to pursue; however, because of Grandfather Hogan's experience and contacts in Southern Africa, I presume they are leaning in that direction.

In addition to that news, Patrick wrote that their old car is on its last leg and they asked if I would be willing to rent the van to them until I get back, if they deal with the insurance and whatever else is required to put it back on the road.

Or, alternatively, would I sell the van to them for the Blue Book price?

Hum...

Well, after thinking about this situation for a few minutes, Michelle and Patrick, I have firmly decided to give the van to you on an as-is-basis, which should actually be in pretty good shape considering the reputation of the mechanic and the faithfulness of the people who have been starting it up on a weekly basis to keep it in shape. And by the way, thank you for performing that service.

Why do this?

Because more than anyone else you two helped to put me on the correct pathway to being a real Christian, which is the greatest thing ever to happen to me, and in some meagre way I want to say thank you for that.

Call it the Church Family Discount.

Marti has the keys and maintenance records, while Leo has the title and my power of attorney, so go see them and I shall warn them you are coming at my behest

------------- ~~~~~~~~~~~ -------------

Okay, now, another set of general questions arose, which are, "Who took the photo of me and the nurse on the helicopter pad?" And "Have I met someone I am interested in?"

Putting the latter question first I reply: emphatically not!

And if I had remembered that shot was on that roll of film I would have cut it out before sending it to Patrick for developing.

Anyway, the nurse in the picture is not only quite bossy (oh man, is she ever!), she is also the fiancee of one of the doctors here, to whom I wish all of the luck in the world to

Just before that photo was snapped by a friend of mine, she was screaming and swearing at me concerning a test which she wanted done STAT, and we all know how much I deeply dislike being yelled and sworn at.

Thankfully she is only a second lieutenant and her signature alone appeared on the request slip, so I did not have to consider it to be a true emergency, or even a standard request, let alone a STAT or even an ASAP request without a doctor's initials.

Still, after she finished her rant, I returned to the lab and ran the test, which turned out to be slightly above normal, indicating that there might have been some sort of a problem that needed attention.

So then I ran a set of associated tests which all turned out normal, meaning "What?"

In any case, she was partly right, and so I put a note in the patient's file suggesting the doctor re-examine his patient and run some duplicate tests to find out if they might show the same results.

Anyway, she is definitely not someone I have any interest in.

------------ ~~~~~~~~~~~~ ------------

Now, to keep up with the changes in the crew as things presently stand:

Bob and Sue have already moved out while Patrick, Michelle, and Marti continue to anchor the house.

But then there is Emmet, the most recent addition to Old House (need a photo for my prayer board).

According to Marti he is about my age, pretty bright, and has an interest in biochemistry.

And Patrick said he has settled into Bob's old room and taken over the job of keeping the downstairs public areas clean and the woodpile stocked, which as a farm boy he should be very at home with.

Thus, there is presently one room open, which is Sue's old room, so I presume that Marti is busy phoning previous female applicants to see who might still be interested in a room.

Or are most people are still not interested because of the separate male and female rooms policy?

Anyway, I presume this is one of the reasons for wondering when I might be home and whether I plan to continue school and moving back into the Roost.

------------ ~~~~~~~~~~~~ ------------

23:15 hrs. - Break for midnight chow.

------------ ~~~~~~~~~~~~ ------------

Day 320 - CRB-RVN

Back in the hooch, as the meds and percolator begin to do their jobs and the clock quietly slips past 00:45 hrs. I am taking a moment to note just where and how we are crossing the threshold of a brand-new week.

The expression which I come up with is, "Oh, what joy! Another seven days filled with the same government-certified blend of political and militaristic feces as always."

No hint of any significant changes drifting by on the wind.

But how do I know that will be the case? Quite simply because that is all there is here inside of this Black Marshmallow dimension, which is a mental and spiritual state of existence in which everyone involved is suspended in an extremely viscous solution where no light penetrates the surface so there is no way to tell, with any degree of certainty, what is going on or who is trapped in it with you.

In other words, the walls of the Dimension act as a communications net designed to keep everyone involved as much in the dark as possible, and it works relatively well.

Of course, now and then a postcard, letter, or even a care package such as this recent one you sent gets through and someone herein receives a message which elevates their spiritual and psychological conditions to a slight degree, at least for a little while.

And if that recipient shares their good fortune with others close to them, which some do, it can potentially elevate those people as well, and help us all to remain aware that beyond this realm of darkness there is yet what we define as normality and personal freedom, somewhere out there beyond the South China Sea.

Thus, we retain some hope that one day we might experience those things again.

In other words, the faith and love which all of you send keeps me from giving in to the cursed marshmallow and sinking deep into hopelessness.

So please continue to write about whatever is on your minds and hearts and I will continue to do the same.

In any case, that is all I have for you as a group for the time being.
Hope this letter is not too much of a bummer and that you will receive it in the intended spirit, which is feeling hopeful and having faith in God, in spite of whatever you are dealing with.

So I ask you not to worry so much about me but instead to pray for the Lord to lead me into a somewhat more optimistic existence wherein my heart, mind, and soul are all in balance, properly focused on doing God's will.

And when you pray, please keep the following rules in mind:
1. There is a God, but none of us are Him.
2. Pray for His will to be done in all of our lives and for us to accept it.
3. You can never have too many people praying for you, so invite others to pray with you.

Your friend and brother in Yeshua Ha'Maschiyach (Jesus the Messiah),

Jake

13. Letter #3 - Day 320
   - Early Sunday Morning

Dear Leo and Kathleen,

04:10 hrs Sunday as I sit here in the common space in the hooch, working on a second pot of thick black coffee, still wide awake and determined to finish this letter, plus one more, if possible, before I surrender to the rack.

This way I can post all of these letters in one bundle, the way you folks did, and they should all be there by this coming Friday.

Leo, you started off by asking if I have heard anything from my mother or Ray since the emancipation proceedings and if so, what they had to say.

Well, in spite of my initial decision not to say anything to you or anyone else about it at the time, now I will tell you about it because you have become my family and I have come to honour you both as parents and know you are only asking because you truly care about me.

Anyway, as it happened, somehow or another Nora managed to acquire my former PO Box number in Collegeville, and shortly after I moved in with you, she wrote to say that Ray and his cohorts had stripped the house of everything of any value and left her to face the consequences of their various illegal activities and for trying to sell the house, which you already know about.

Thus, she was in need of more money than what she makes working at the restaurant and asked if I could help her out.

Thankfully, I had steamed the envelope open as a precaution, so after reading it I resealed it and marked it, "Not at this Address, Return to Sender," then closed out the PO Box without leaving any sort of forwarding address.

Thankfully, since that one attempt to reach me I have not heard anything from or about either her or Ray, nor do I care to regardless of the circumstances.

So, why are you asking about them?

What have they done now?

------------ ~~~~~~~~~~~~ ------------

Kathleen, you asked if anything went on between me and Sue shortly after I moved into Old House.

In response to that question I can honestly tell you, the entire crew and the person who started this rumour that nothing of any nature has gone on between me and anyone else at any point since I moved in with you folks or ever before that.

However, there was a not-so-pleasant misunderstanding which occurred during my second week at Old House.

Which is to say, at the suggestion of a very troubled soul named James, Sue was led to believe that I wanted to take her out but was too shy to ask.

So she sent me a note stating that she was open to the idea of dating me and all I need do was to ask.

Of course, that was news to me, so I responded, but unfortunately in a rather undiplomatic fashion, by telling her straightaway that I like her as a friend; however, I was not interested in any other type of relationship with anyone, for any reason, which was true at that time but not too smooth.

In response to that, for some time afterwards she refused to speak to me and even returned a paper that I was paying her to edit with a comment attached which read, "Ask someone else to correct your lousy writing."

Fortunately, a few weeks after Bob moved in, and they became interested in each other, and soon thereafter Sue apologized, and since then we have been very good friends, plus she has edited a lot of my work since then.

Anyway, that is the straight story and I hope it helps to resolve whatever questions you have about this matter.

Next there is a triptych of questions which no doubt stem from information provided from the same unscrupulous source.

Question one: did I drop both of my correspondence courses and cancel the haematology paper I was working on?

Question two: what are my plans for the summer and fall terms?

Question three: do I know that Marti has moved from her room on second floor into the Roost, presumably to keep it safe in case I fail to re-register for classes by the fall?

Given the nature of these questions, I suspect that James the Jerk still works part time in the registrar's office and thereby has come to know that I dropped those classes and have not yet requested info for any future terms.

It all lines up with his spiteful nature, and I believe he still wants revenge for losing the coin toss for the Roost to me and then for being booted out of the co-op for snooping about other people's room and being a thief.

Wherever he goes that guy is a problem child who simply refuses to accept the fact that he causes his own problems and is the one who needs to change, not the world around him.

In any case, to be honest I am a bit surprised that Marti would move into the Roost, without first notifying me about the apparent problem, listing the best options, and asking which one I prefer to pursue, as that has been her lawyer-like routine ever since I have known her.

Anyway, if I get this correctly, Marti caught wind of the fact that I recently dropped my correspondence courses and having made no inquiry about registering for classes next fall, theoretically blows my grade average and student status away, making me ineligible to remain at Old House.

However, it does not offer any answers as to why I dropped those classes, nor what I plan to do in their place or have done to deal with the problem.

Well, the fact is, along with my request to drop those classes I sent a letter to each instructor and to my guidance counsellor which explained my present situation along with copies of my medical records and that I am requesting a sabbatical for mental health reasons.

Those letters also mentioned that when I finally return I want to change my course of studies from Science and Medicine to English, Poetry, Fine Arts, Philosophy and Religious Studies.

These are changes that I hope and pray will help me to overcome those things which have been affecting me in such a negative manner for some time now.

So please be informed what you were told about me dropping classes was less than half of the truth, and as I still have time to formally report all of this to the co-op board, so there is actually no reason to panic.

------------ ~~~~~~~~~~~~ ------------

Now I have a question for the two of you, asking in advance that you not mention or even hint about this matter to your daughter because whenever I do finally get home and speak to her about it, I want it to be somewhat of a surprise.

Also, please know that I have seriously considered and prayed about how my past and present situations have affected me, hoping that I will not be any sort of burden to you or to Marti at any point, now or in the future.

Anyway, now that you have known me for a few years and have had sufficient time to assess my usual state of mind and willingness to work to improve my personal situation and relationships, I am asking for your permission to ask Marti out on an actual date.

At the same time I promise if either one of you disapproves of this, for any reason, at anytime, I shall not pursue the matter any further.

So, is it all right with you both and do you think she will agree to it?
Thank you both for being all that you are to me and may God richly bless you for it.

Oh yes, and Kathleen, thank for the poetry books and the cassette.

Most Sincerely,

Jake

Truth Must Be Sought

14. Letter #4 -Day 320 continued -

Dear Bob and Sue,

It is just approaching 07:30 hrs and so I should have time to knock out a couple of pages before hitting the rack for a few hours.

As you know, this secondary reply to your letters is about dealing with the personal comments and questions, which in your case are focused on my writing, artwork, and whether or not I have carefully considered your argument for publishing some of those pieces, in order to educate people and influence their understanding of this and other armed conflicts.

Of course, I honestly believe that I have been open-minded while considering your many requests to use my works in said manner.

In fact, I have even meditated on and prayed for spiritual insight concerning this matter.

Although I cannot claim that my reasons for not doing this are any more logical than your reasons for doing it, I must still refuse, at least for the time being.

First of all, as previously stated, I do not want to infect anyone else with the disgusting ungodly reality of this situation, or to accuse any innocent people of willingly supporting it.

As previously stated, I believe there are many people here and at home who are not particularly evil, but just misguided, and I feel that screaming at them, even with truth in hand, will not change their hearts and minds.

Yes, change does require that the truth be told, but it must be delivered with love. (Read: 1 Corinthians chapter 13).

Why? Because all people (all of us included) are sinful, ignorant, stubborn, vengeful souls, who insist on continuing along the broad pathway of human history rather than admitting we are all desperately in need of God's forgiveness and guidance, because only God's pure love can help us to see and accept the truth.

So at least for now I must continue to decline to publish any of my personal experiences from here inside the Black Marshmallow.

These writings and drawings are merely bits and pieces of my personal journal, and at best, they tell an incomplete story.

However, your requests to air some of my poems on the college radio station and to publish them in the *Back Alley* is a possibility, *if* we can agree upon certain points which must be stated in writing and signed by both of you and whoever is in charge at the radio station, prior to my reading them, *after* I am a civilian once again.

These points are as follows:
    1. I shall retain all rights to and full control of my work and be guaranteed that the pieces will be aired in whole, without any commentary from anyone else, so that the audience can decide for themselves what to think of them.

    2. My real name and current situation must *not* be mentioned, and I will be referred to only as "the author."

    3. The radio station shall be responsible for

recording and airing my readings, but no one will edit them following my approval of the finished product, without my personal written permission and immediate oversight.

4. It shall be my sole responsibility to select three poems to be recorded and possibly published along with one drawing.

5. Of course, after recording them you have the right to refuse to air and/or publish them if you so desire.

And now for a final comment concerning any and all questions about my feelings for Marti, I will simply paraphrase and old song lyric which simply states "it ain't nobody's business but my own." Love you both and pray for you on a regular basis,
Jake

15. Letter #5 -Day 321 - CRB-RVN

Dear Patrick and Michelle,

It is currently approaching 0300 hrs Monday morning, which is approximately fifteen hours, if my often-questionable math skills are correct, after I finished writing letters to the whole crew, and personal ones to Leo and Kathleen, plus to Spitfire Sue and Big Bob.

Do to the fact that after that marathon writing session it was necessary to take some time to sleep for an extended period and then to take care of some personal business such as getting some laundry together for our hooch maid who will be here later this morning and to double check my schedule and get some chow.

In any case, to start with I want to comment on the news about Grandfather Hogan having passed away, which I am very sorry to hear about, especially because it sounds as if it was a difficult matter at the end with the cancer and all.

Yet he left this world on such a magnificent note, praising the Lord in spite of all his pain and suffering.

The first true Christian, college graduate, physician, and missionary in your family, he certainly blazed a wonderful path for you both to follow.

So let me begin by offering you both some encouragement with an early congrats for being so close to your long-term goals of becoming a doctor and registered nurse, husband and wife team, and for starting to nail down what mission field you plan to practice in, at least to start with.

Personally, as you can see, I too am coming ever closer to my present goal of becoming a civilian, if I read the tea leaves correctly.

And yes, that will include *not* being a lab technician any longer.

As you can tell from the letter to the whole crew, I simply cannot see continuing in the medical field.

Too many bodies and too much blood, venereal disease, sickle cell anaemia, leukemia, malaria, Agent Orange, and such.

Who knows, perhaps I will take up planning civil rights and anti-war educational courses or perhaps become a cloistered monk of sorts and live in the north woods where I can make maple syrup and raise honeybees.

Or I could take up writing poetry and doing calligraphy as a full time profession, and starve to death in a cold-water flat somewhere in Eastern Europe, hoping that my works sell for a small fortune after I die.

Anyway, let us get off this little rabbit trail and back to reality.

Tomorrow is my appointment to be re-X-rayed, see the shrink, and take some psych tests, which should give him somewhat of a better idea of what is going on with me, or so I hope.

As stated in the initial letter to the entire crew, his preliminary guess is that I am suffering from combat fatigue or something of that nature.

While I believe I am simply massively depressed from too much pernicious crap and am in desperate need of a few of years of R&R.

Also, I want you both to know that I have indeed become truly interested in reading and formally studying the Word and possibly some Greek so that I can read the New Testament in the original language and thereby get more out of it.

Not that I have suddenly become a student of ancient languages, but I would like to take a course or two at some Bible College and at least give the Greek thing a shot.

Anyway, have you ever read or heard this
little limerick?

There once was a curate from Peru
Who kept a small cat in a pew
He taught it to speak
Alphabetical Greek
But it never got further than μ (mew)

Okay, it is somewhat of a groaner and there
are several versions of it, but I like this
one the best.

And now a couple of notes concerning the van:

As previously stated, Marti has the keys
and maintenance records, while Leo has the
registration and insurance records plus my power
of attorney.

Then, too, its summer tires are at Hector's place,
and you should definitely have him check it over
as it has been sitting for a while, and because we
know that he is an honest top-notch mechanic,
especially when it comes to imports.

------------ ~~~~~~~~~~~ ------------

Finally, I have a real poem for you, which is
now yours and therefore you may do as you wish
with it.

It is titled "My Father's House" and it was inspired by a small church that I saw standing in the midst of an area that had been heavily shelled but, miraculously, not hit even once, as far as I could tell from the road.

In any case, I composed it as a folk hymn, with Michelle's voice and guitar style in mind, but whether it can be used as a set of lyrics or not is strictly your call.

Hope that you will like it.

Your friend and brother in Christ,

Jake

My Father's House

My Father's house is humble
Made of bricks of straw and mud
It stands out on the battle field
Soaked in tears and sweat and blood
A refuge to the inocent
Hatred cannot reach
And loving hearts may call their home
This monument to peace

My Father's House is precious
Filled with golden dreams
Standing amid fertile fields
Cultivated and serene
Surrounded by creation
Filled with truths untold
A school of enlightenment
Where great mysteries unfold

My Father's House is common
Made of tissue, hair and bone
My Father's House is sacred
Its full worth to seldom known
My Father's House is cosmic
It holds the planets, moons and suns
My Father's House can be any house
Or the heart of anyone ~

SEVENEAU

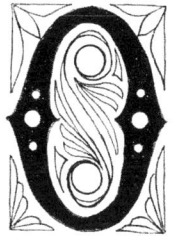

16. Letter #6 - Day 321 - CRB-RVN

My Dearest Marti,

It is 0630 hrs. Monday morning and, although I am not on duty today, I am sitting in the Blood Bank determined to finish this letter to you and get the whole bundle of letters into the post by noon today.

As you know, I always save the best for last and because you are the best...

First and foremost, I want to tell you that no matter what, you have been, are now and will always be my best friend, so whatever I say to you here is being said out of a deep desire to see our relationship grow and flower in whatever manner God wants it to.

Also, you should know that whatever rumours that someone (probably James) has been spreading about me are deliberately fictitious and designed to try and destroy our friendship.

And for clarification of that fact, you should consult with your parents as I have explained in some detail what is really happening concerning my student status and future plans.

Furthermore, part of that is the blatant lie that seems to be circulating which says that something went on between myself and Sue shortly after I moved from your parents' place into Old House.

The fact is nothing whatsoever has ever gone on between me and anyone else ever, except for the kisses I gave you upon leaving for boot camp and then again when I was at home on leave preparing for Phase II Tech School.

And now that has been said, I must admit to feeling like chewing you out for risking your position as manager of the co-operative by trying to cover up for my personal problems.

Okay, "chewing you out" is far too harsh a term.

So please allow me to rephrase that and just say that I want to talk to you about having moved yourself into the Roost to cover up for me not completing my correspondence courses this semester, which may seemingly makes me ineligible to claim student status and continue residing at Old House.

But even if that were to happen, it is not really so terrible, is it?

After all I can still live somewhere close to OH or just outside town near the farmstead.

In other words, this thing would not condemn me to life back out on the streets or being able to attend school whenever I finally get out of here.

Plus, since my grandmother's house sold I can definitely afford to move my belongings into some warehouse, or better yet back to your folks' place if they would agree to it, which I am fairly certain they would.

In any case, I understand why you did what you have done and am extremely grateful, because I hope to return to school with a new major, when I am a civilian once more.

But at the moment, I am definitely incapable of continuing the previous course of study, which is why I quit working on the correspondence courses and paper on malaria.

And you know, had you asked me about the situation, I would have confessed and asked you to plead my case before the board, which I am certain would have taken the heat off of you.

Jake Seveneau

Nonetheless, we are now where we are with this issue, and so I suggest we initiate the following plan for a formal hearing, unless, of course, you have a better idea.

Naturally, as you are already involved and therefore cannot sit in your usual board seat during said hearing, you are the ideal person to speak for me.

As previously stated, when writing to your parents I have already written formal letters, signed by the local shrink, concerning the fact I am suffering from a psychological disorder and thus am no longer equipped to study, so that I clearly need a sabbatical for at least six months to one year to be treated for and to overcome this problem.

And since the board accepted my time in technical school as full-time study, I cannot see why they should reject this plea.

------------ ~~~~~~~~~~~ ------------

Now, too, as you already know from reading the group letter, I am giving the van to Patrick and Michelle, so please give them the keys and maintenance records concerning it and please see they go to your father to obtain the registration and insurance papers.

Also, before they drive off in it, please have them stand in the back yard with the house in the background and take a couple of photos of them, in full hippie regalia beside the van for my scrapbook.

------------ ~~~~~~~~~~~ ------------

Finally, I have been thinking about our personal relationship the whole time I have been working on these letters and pretty much ever since we met, and in consideration of it I have decided to include another poem which I wrote with you in mind.
In fact, it is about you, so please know that it is now yours and you may do whatever you wish with it.

Your friend and occasional source of annoyance,

Jake

PS. Ask Sue to play some Taj Mahal for me on her Sunday night broadcast.

Mariah

17. Mariah

Amid the fertile rolling hills
along the banks of a meandering stream
in a daylight dream she appears

Disguised as a gentle summer breeze
caressing body, mind, and soul
sending every fear away

Lifting me up so far beyond self
beyond every attachment to reality
the limits of human dreams

onto a plane of unnameable colours
within an aurora of unimaginable energy

We float as clouds
dance as lightning
shimmer as stars
then drift back to earth
as autumn leaves

Where with a final touch of grace
she disappears

Leaving me with but a memory
questions and prayers

about everything

18. Camouflaged Nightmares

Myths such as we are God's ordained
the police force unto the world
and war is occasionally necessary
are things I never quite understood

Still near the age of majority
with many who believed such things
I was essentially conscripted
ordered to march
to do what is righteous
enforce the rules of capitalism
demonstrate proper civilization
unto the lost
for God 'n' country
family and friends

So we trained then traveled hither and yon
until reaching the battlefield
where slowly but surely
reality educated us all

through varied experiences only hell could arrange
such as "friendly" fire
fallen comrades by the dozen
and the unexpected factor of collateral damage
so many civilians wounded and dead

orphaned children
other foul and ungodly things

Things one cannot simply leave behind
forget about
like the ribbons and medals one hides in a drawer
or in the pages of a journal written for posterity
roughly composed and filed away

Because these bits of reality
are like beetle wasps
which bore down deep into one's soul
and deposit their eggs

leaving their spawn to develop surreptitiously
slowly eating their way to the surface
until the time is ripe

Then suddenly they tear into the open
reminding us of all that we have taken part in

and every time I suffer guilt and anxiety
over and over
again and again

Causing decade's worth of writhing with cold
reality
uncertainty

Sometimes running up and down
back and forth
turning and churning

racing manically
along the open road
or
meandering from place to place
job to job
thought to thought

Sometimes sitting silently for hours
in darkened corners
or hiding in the wilderness
for weeks on end

generally unable to deal with relationships
to focus on the present

Until suicide becomes appealing
but only leads to the Psychotropic Lounge
an extensive trip through the DSM
revolving logic and musical couches

Another game designed and operated
by the same con artists who composed the myths
we are God's ordained
the police force unto the world
and war is occasionally necessary

And now it is four decades hence
one sliver of hope remains

to forcefully extract this offensive mass
this masticated curio of
sword and pen

blood and ink
flesh and paper

and publish as much of it as I can stand to
for my own good
God 'n' country
family and friends
and perhaps a few others

who might come to understand without repeating my errors
and with an open heart pray
God will forgive us all

Camouflaged Nightmares

19. Journal Entry - 28 August 1971
483rd USAF Hospital - CRB-RVN

To describe my present psychological and spiritual conditions I would use a few key words such as exhausted, nervous, and frightened.

For the past two days I have been doing my regular job in the lab during the day and riding with SSgt. Townes on the SAT jeep at night.

This is something no other medics here do, save Herbert and me, since Turner and Beaucage both DEROSED.

As for us medics, we simply try to stay out of the way and offer some assurance to those who risk their lives throughout every day to guard us.

In other words, we look out for each other in a wide variety of ways.

Anyway, three days ago, early on the morning of Wednesday, 25 August, the Tri-service munitions dump was hit by some sappers who attacked it and managed to set off several large bombs which caused a number of secondary explosions and scattered tons of smaller munitions all over the place.

So for two days now there have been small fires throughout the dump and occasional explosions, but today the mess is starting to calm down a bit.

It makes me think that in the time I have been here at CRB, which is supposed to be a relatively safe base, how the place has been rocketed at least three times and now has suffered this major attack, so it really does not seem all that safe to me.

In my experience, it is just as bad as Nha Trang, where I was before this.

Anyway, thank the Lord this is now Sunday, as I need to sleep for a few hours to recharge my brain and allow my nerves to calm down a bit, if that is possible.

Earlier yesterday, Saturday morning I was on the SAT jeep with SSgt. Townes, who is the one I usually ride with, when we stopped for EOD to guide us through an area where munitions were scattered all around, and while we stood beside the jeep, an unexpected blast knocked me backwards so that I slammed my head against the vehicle and as a result was unconscious for a minute or so.

Thank the Lord I had a helmet on, per Townes' insistence, as it likely kept me from having a much more serious injury.

So after being examined and X-rayed, the doctor said I probably would not suffer any permanent damage.

That is little comfort considering that others have suffered more or lost their lives as a result of this recent attack.

Some guard towers and small buildings have been destroyed, plus at least eight people that I now know about have been killed.

Of course, that is very little on the overall scale of all the deaths and injuries which have occurred as a result of this "police action," especially if you count all of the casualties on both sides.

And most definitely it is more hell than I ever wanted to see or hear about.

Still, I am exhausted, nervous and frightened as a result of this one small experience, and I probably will be for many days to come.

So what must it be like for those who live in the very heart of this Camouflaged Nightmare?

It does the same things to every soul involved
until the whole truth comes out between the
partners and then requests for some come in to do
something like forcing the authorities to take
notes about us while trying to explain

20. Sandpiper

(For soprano or alto voice with flute accompaniment)

Note: In spite of all the crap going on, there are a few occasional moments of sanity and even of genuine happiness which occur.

Sandpiper…Sandpiper…
Sandpiper, sing me your song
Sing it to me all day long

See the sandpipers on the beach
playing all the day
in the foaming surf they dance
to the rhythm of the waves

Sandpiper, sing me your song
Sing to me all day long

Float upon the gentle air
pleasant melodies
Softly as the earth goes round
soothing symphonies

Sandpiper… Sandpiper…
Sandpiper, sing me your song
Sing it to me all day long

21. Journal Entry - 18 October 1971
483rd USAF Hospital - CRB-RVN

Having worked Monday night, I had Tuesday off and so spent it accompanying Dr. Carlson on a MEDCAP run into town.

In the morning we went to the local orphanage and then to the clinic in Cam Rahn village where, guided by a local physician, we saw a dozen or so patients and all went well until the very end of the day.

Unfortunately, the last patient on the ward was a young girl of about fifteen or sixteen by my best guess, whom I looked in on by mistake.

Later on, I was told that she had been found in an alley, severely beaten, raped and then burned.

Judging from her response to me, I would guess that her attackers were G. I.s and probably Caucasian, as she did not freak out when the Vietnamese doctor or nurse were in sight, but the instant she set eyes on me she became terrified and began to scream like a banshee, as if reliving the events that put her there and she did not stop screaming for several minutes after the Vietnamese nurse and Doctor Carlson hustled me off down the corridor until I was out of her sight.

What happened to her is so horrendous, so unimaginable, that I still cannot believe it is even possible for anyone to even think of doing, let alone to actually do something of that nature to anyone else?

Of course, I do not even understand the type of war where two armies just shoot back and forth at each other, so forget about trying to comprehend this level of complete rabid madness.

After my encounter with the girl, the Vietnamese doctor tried to explain her condition to me and, as he spoke, all of the crap I have seen the past several months came rushing back into my mind, like a freight train filled with explosives that blew me out into the street, in one elongated blast, and tore my mind and heart into bloody shreds.

From the dead woman and badly wounded little boy I saw on my first day at Nha Trang, to the incident at the ammo dump in late August, to this poor tortured girl, it all came back like napalm tearing through a village and as a result I simply lost it.

Feelingviolently nauseous, I ran outside to the ambulance, and kneeling beside it, I spewed an

extensive load of vomit into the street.
Then, after a bit, I crawled into the ambulance and wept aggressively until Carlson came out.

Then, even though I was starting to recover, he gave me a shot of something fairly strong to keep me calm as we drove back to base.

The saddest part of all this is that, as far as I am concerned, there are many people who see the same stuff I do but do not seem to comprehend its depth and what it says about humanity.

They look right at people like that girl and say, "it sucks," but that is all.

They do not seem personally affected by it in their own souls.

It is almost as if in their minds they are not even here, but at home watching a movie.

They do not see that any of these people could be their family, or that the girl there in the clinic could just as well be their sister, mother, or daughter.

They do not need to vomit and cry out to God for mercy or forgiveness, which I find extremely strange.

It is as if they lack something, as if some disease has literally consumed their humanity. But I suppose that is why war is possible in the first place.

Because there are some people who can go into the field and not feel what is happening to others in the deepest part of their souls.

Or perhaps there is something wrong with me.

Maybe I feel too much.

It is true that just about everything I come in contact with here feels as though it is either happening to me and it is my own fault.

Is that wrong?

Should I not feel this agony and guilt?

22. War is About Children

War is about children
baptized with its fire
whose families are torn asunder
disintegrated
murdered
whose homes are overrun
burned
bombed
masticated by the beast of hatred
turned into moonscapes

all before their once innocent eyes
until they have been so damaged outside and in
they can never be children again

War is about children
baptized in its name
born to girls still children themselves
the victims of prostitution
of rape

Children left at an orphanage gate
hidden by their mothers
because they cannot care for them
because they will find only prejudice in the world

because their male parents will only deny or laugh
them off

Not because of their sin
but because they remind us of ours

War is about children
baptized in the silence of its hollow heart
whose siblings or parents no longer laugh or play
but just sit alone
weeping in the dark
screaming in their sleep
their hearts and minds deeply wounded
forever scarred

Yes
War is about children
yours and mine
baptized to speak its truth
because they know much more than they should

War is About Children

23. Journal Entry - 10 December 1971
483rd USAF Hospital - CRB-RVN

Today was a bit Dantesque in my mind in that it contained some symbolism blended with the harsh realities of war.

The symbolism was a toy soldier glued to the dashboard of a jeep which I was assigned to use in delivering some units of blood and plasma to a small clinic just up the road.

Then too there was the reality was a severed foot still contained in a tattered combat boot which I was unexpectedly ordered to bring back to the pathology department here at the 483rd for examination and possible identification.

All of this began early this morning as I was loading the cooler filled with blood and plasma into the jeep, when I first noticed the little olive drab draftee lying in a prone position, semi-perpendicular to the centre post of the dashboard, pointing his rifle through the right side of the windscreen toward the road ahead.

Naturally, I did not particularly care for it as it rubbed against my CO sensibilities.

Nonetheless, over here some guys decorate stuff in strange ways for all sorts of reasons and the rule of thumb is if it is not actually harming something, it is best to leave it alone, so I did, and therefore when driving away my initial thoughts had nothing to do with the little plastic figurine.

Instead, I was primarily concerned about making it out and back in less than three hours if the road was clear and the ROK and ARVN guard posts did not jerk me around too much, which they rarely do when one is driving an ambulance or medical jeep, especially if you are transporting a cooler full of blood and plasma.

Unfortunately, on the way out I met up with a US Army convoy that was traveling at twenty-five kilometres max, so it took well more than an hour just getting there and throughout that stop and go ride I had not one thought about the little toy.

Then when I finally arrived at the clinic the NCOIC, hearing I was from the 483rd, decided it was the perfect opportunity to get rid of the frozen foot which had been taking up space in their freezer for several days prior to that.

Of course, upon reading the description and seeing it as they placed it in the cooler and poured a load of ice on top, I was quite reluctant to accept the assignment, but an order is an order, and so I took it onboard and left there in begrudging silence.

On the way back there were no major holdups, just the two road posts and some heightened traffic in the villages which barely slowed me down.

Still, as I traveled along and shifted up and down the cooler slid around on the passenger side floor and thus I was continually distracted by it and forced to think of that detached foot and in time that foot and the toy soldier took on a new significance for me.

In fact, they soon triggered a series of unpleasant thoughts, beginning with the fact I was a fool not to have gone to Canada instead of volunteering to serve as a medic.

Then too came a series of memories of all the insane crap that I have witnessed over here and, somehow, I could imagine the modern plastic soldier with its sophisticated weapon turning into a tin soldier with a musket, then into a wooden soldier on a chariot with bow and spear, then finally into a caveman with a stick and a rock.

It went all the way back to a time when one of Cain's close relatives was encouraging his children to practice killing their neighbours while he told them how they were honour bound to serve their household, to defend against any and all aggressors and conquer those who were targets for expansion.

In other words, I could suddenly see how the little soldier was a mechanism for training young boys to become government-sanctioned killers.

It went from being a simple piece of plastic to a thorn in my mind, a type of wicked seed that takes root as a lie that one's family and nation are the best and deserve to be defended and to own more crap than any other nation, including all that belongs to one's neighbours…

So much for the second great commandment.

This is the birth of pride and prejudice, the birth of colonialism and manifest destiny.

Over that stretch of road, weaving through the small villages and checkpoints I came to see the connection between the toy soldier and the real soldier's severed foot.

Plus I saw that the connection cannot be completely broken as long as people possess fallen natures; still, I prayed quietly for the moral strength to break my personal connection to these things.

Then, after delivering the foot to pathology, I snuck off to do something semi-realistic to help soothe my tortured mind.

Driving down to the beach beside Tiger Rock and parking there, I took a scalpel from my field kit and did some field surgery on the olive drab figurine by freeing it from the dashboard and then removing its rifle and helmet.

After which I tied the newly created little civilian to a piece of driftwood and set him afloat on the outgoing tide.

Now here I sit at the Seaman's Club, writing this down in my journal while waiting for my tea to cool and thinking that one possible title for my memoir might be, "It was the Little Things."

24. Toy Soldiers

They pick us out in mass quantities
as if we came by the gross
in plastic bags

They put us in harm's way
damage us
toss us aside
little toys
a dime a dozen

disposable playthings
pawns on the chessboard

Our only purpose to be cannon fodder
silage for animals

25. Evil Fog

Can any human being
heart or mind
any relationship
family or friendship
withstand this grief
this anger
fear and confusion

Can any even comprehend
this insidious
invisible poison ether

this evil fog
drifting over the earth
coming and going wherever it will
slithering and dining on our souls
like a Burmese python

gluttonously consuming hope and faith
love and life
defecating naught but despair
and disloyalty
hate and death
leaving behind trails of desolation
wherever it goes

Can any outmanoeuvre its ominous flow
resist its powerful coils
survive its aftermath

26. Infinite Burdens

It begins with a trickle
a tiny stream

One by land
two by sea
a few by air

and naturally we have no fear
we have the foremost technology
have been well trained
are experienced at our craft

One is nothing
two simple
even a dozen are not too many

but the flow is constant
and as trickles form streams
streams form rivers
producing more wounded
more torn and broken
burned and poisoned
crushed by reality
each one carrying another

One score for mending
two for surgery
three in search of sanity
four for miraculous resurrection

so we stack them up in waiting piles
then number
triage
treat and ship them

while the waiting piles expand
and still they come
a gross by day
a ton by night
begging
pleading
needing us
until we are beaten down and broken
crushed by reality
wailing and babbling in the moonlight

We are not gods, you morbid bastards
we are nothing more than flesh and blood
Have pity on us, please
have pity

but still they come

Infinite Burden

27. Women Too

Men are not the only ones here
there are many women too

Local women
some old
some young
many just girls

They fill homes and public spaces
cities and villages
desperately holding together whatever
remains of their families
of their homeland
their sanity

A few have the rare privilege of living moral
lives
But many are hooch maids by day
butterflies by night

Others are slaves sold to brothel owners
forced to do things no one should
praying to survive the triple hell of their prison

All are trapped in this bloody mess

Then, too, there are the women from outside
mostly volunteers
only God knows why

A few stewardesses
who come and go
some Red Cross Doughnut Dollies
at least one radio host

and several nurses
who make it look and sound
a bit like home
which I am uncertain is good or bad

Another thing I have noticed

All are forced to develop their strengths
courage
wisdom
as quickly as possible

So they are far more mature than they first appear
and all work as hard as any man
probably harder
and some do so while carrying children
or some man
who cannot or will not carry themselves
because they're infirmed apron clinger

These women work in hospitals
shops
offices

fields
boats
and sadly
regrettably
some become soldiers
pawns of the men behind the killing

So it seems like with the men
a few are mostly good
others bad
all confused
trapped in the very centre of Dante's nightmare

In any case, I just thought you might want to know
men are not the only ones here
there are women too

28. Row After Row

Row after row the hooches stand
plywood huts with metal roofs
where we try to sleep on cots of steel
in beds that we ourselves have made

Row after row of metal Quonsets stand
along a partly sheltered walk
from outside they appear innocuous

some might even think they are merely respites
for the sick and wounded
but inside
row after row the beds are filled with truth

the names and faces of the deceived
pawns in a bloody struggle to decide
which king's name will go first in a history book
victor or vanquished

Row after row lights shine down on reality
who can close their eyes
look away
from row after row
of evidence

29. Enemies

Wounded
Stitched up and bandaged
              with two IVs
              in full restraints

Separated from the others
by a missing bed
   a Korean guard
   skin pigmentation
   language
   politics
   et cetera

As every eye wanders back and forth
              his and theirs
              curiously
              suspicious and uneasy
as hatred and ignorance brews then cools
then brews again

some towards us as we do our jobs
       because we do our jobs
obeying the oath to do no harm

Jake Seveneau

Perhaps these enemies will leave here
still filled with hate
still blaming each other for their loses

Perhaps we (the medics, nurses and doctors)
should all just pack up and leave

let them do whatever they want to each other
let them bind their own bloody wounds
perhaps the war would end much sooner
But that is not how some of us treat our enemies
Matthew 5:43-48

30. Midnight Mercy Plane

Flew into hell's own aftermath on the midnight mercy plane
Scrawled upon the wall of death, thought I saw your name

Refusing to accept it I went and found you there
laid beneath a bloody sheet wearing a vacant stare

As those low dark clouds came rolling in again
to claim another innocent young man

At times I wish that they would come for me
to terminate the madness and end the agony

Perhaps it would be better than living to recall
the wounded and the dead I could do nothing for

and the loved ones who must suffer what I feel every time
those low dark clouds come rolling down the line

There was no time to weep just then or compose a eulogy
living souls were crying out—there were wounds to treat

Still all that I could think of is what lured you there
to offer others comfort and help reduce their pain

But those low dark clouds came rolling by again
to claim another innocent young man

At times I wish that they would come for me
to terminate the madness and end the agony

Perhaps it would be better than living to recall
the wounded and the dead I could do nothing for

and the loved ones who must suffer what I feel every time
those low dark clouds come rolling down the line

31. Merry Christmas, 1971

This day we celebrate the birth of Messiah
                        the Prince of Peace

In His honour
our leaders have declared a cease fire

so today we pledge not to bomb innocent villagers
                    to spray them with defoliant

In honour of God's only begotten Son

Just as we pledge not to have any other gods
not to take His name in vain
to remember the Sabbath and keep it holy
to honour our mothers and fathers
not to murder
not to steal
not to covet our s neighbour's wives
              or neighbour's goods

at least for today
one special day
but not for tomorrow

Jake Seveneau

Tomorrow we shall return to the war
kill in His name
and bomb
    rape
    spill blood in His name

but for right now…

Merry Christmas to all
        and to all a good night

32. Black Marshmallow Dimension

Lingering scents
echoing sounds
randomly jig sawn images
shards of suddenly exploded prayers

All diligently collected
secured in an opaque
thought-proof container
to await a day of sunlight
of hope
when they might be looked at
reassembled
examined
without potentially hazardous emotions
should I survive this howling madness

But long before such a day could appear
the contents combusted spontaneously
erupted like lava from the home of Vulcan

melting flesh and paper
blood and ink
breath and words

creating an unearthly alloy entity
an unnatural curio

Jake Seveneau

unquestionably unstable
left to smoulder
to cool
to form a solid shell

encasing this black marshmallow dimension
absent of light
incredibly viscous
inescapable

where the gatherer has been trapped ever since
meditating on possible purposes
fearing it may be no more than accidental
pure chance
or worse yet, fate

while he prays for light to fracture the shell
for God to release him from its history

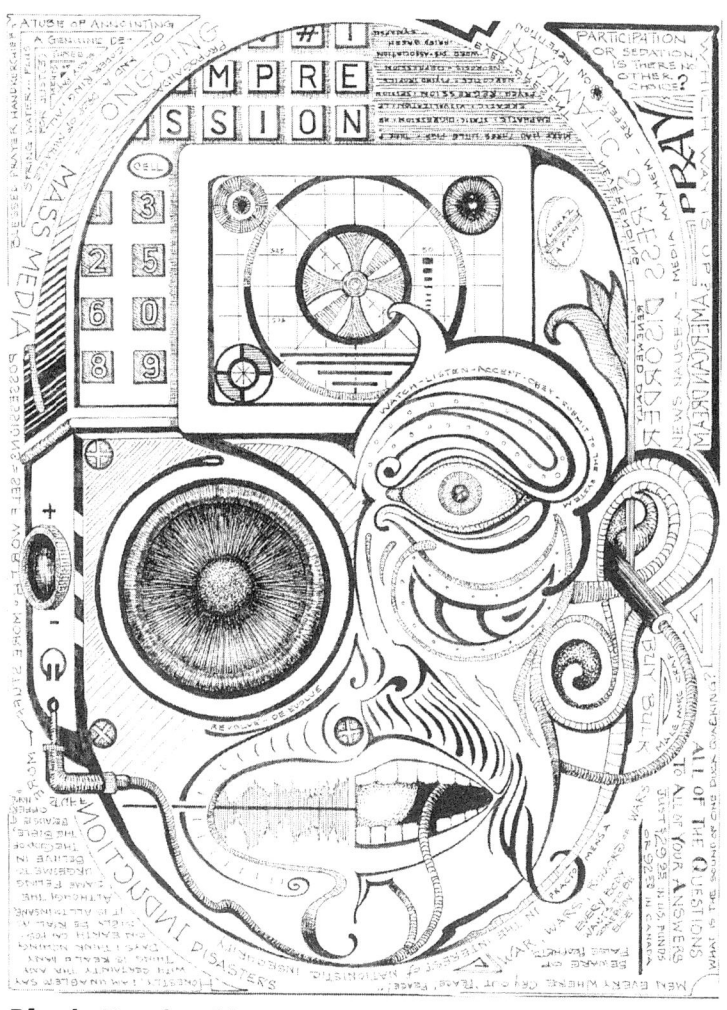

Black Marshmallow Dimension

33. Journal Entry - 29 February 1972
From Ton Son Nhut to Travis

Leap Day 1972 and here I sit in Ton Son Nhut, RVN, just outside Saigon, waiting to board a flight for Travis AFB, California, my next and hopefully final assignment in the USAF.

The orders tucked inside of my briefcase state that I am to report to David Grant Medical Centre there for further examination.

What they do not say is that for whatever reason it has been recommended that I receive an Honourable Discharge under General Conditions, rather than a Medical Discharge.

It is my guess that they are playing it that way, simply saying I am no longer able to fulfill my duties, in order to keep me from getting a disability pension.

Not that I am really worried about it but just hope they do not keep me in the hospital for too long, as more than anything else I desperately want to go home and be with my adoptive family and especially with Marti, whom I love so deeply.

Of course, in addition to that, I would very much like to see Leo and Kathleen and the rest of the Old House Crew whom I also miss: Bob, Sue, Patrick, and Michelle.

Then too I am interested in registering to take a class or two during the summer quarter and then for full-time studies in the fall.

But, not for any medical or science classes, just along the lines of Writing, Literature, Poetry, Art, Philosophy, and Theology, not aiming directly at any degree but simply to learn more about God and His will for my life.

Anyway, I have to fold this up as they are calling for us to board the plane.

PART 3
After

34. Journal Entry - The Ides of March

Here on the psych ward for almost a month now, but to be perfectly honest there is no real change in my condition except for what the meds are doing to relax me so I am not having any panic attacks and am sleeping at least six hours a night without waking up but perhaps once just to use the head.

Otherwise, it is just about like Nam; having nightmares nearly every night and existing in the Black Marshmallow where every day is like the one before and no one knows when or if they will ever get out of here.

The shrinks here have had me take all of the same tests they gave me at CRB twice now and during the day we have what is called "group therapy," although I do not find it very therapeutic.

We just sit in a circle, taking turns talking about whatever is bothering us and of course, it is pretty much the same crap every day.

In truth, I feel that is just re-infecting my brain every twenty-four hours, which makes no sense whatsoever.

How in the heck is that sort of routine supposed to help anyone get over something that has been eating at their soul for nearly three years, from boot camp to Nam and back?

Sometimes I try to talk about that particular point and tell them that discharging me would be a far more helpful move, but of course they disagree and simply mutter various supposedly reassuring phrases.

Other times I have tried talking about more positive things such as repentance, forgiveness, and loving our enemies, but every time I start the nurse or someone else tells me that "religious propaganda" is inappropriate in this place.

That and the few times when I have tried to quietly pray or read my Bible, one of the two real jerks here has come along and purposely interrupted me.

Of course, in reality, that is insane because the only one who can and will heal any of us is God, but these barbarians simply do not get that.

In fact, they fear it and so they vehemently deny it.

My final point for this session, which is a good one, is that today I have been given permission to use my typewriter for a half hour each day after evening chow as therapy, so long as the young Dr. Kildare (my shrink) can read whatever I write.

And that is the primary reason I am being so honest and to the point herein, so he will possibly come to understand where I am coming from and what I truly need.

But now I am being told that my thirty minutes are up and so I must go.

35. Difficult Choices

Senses, aptitude, the ability to reason
conscience, freewill, a number of seasons

historical knowledge, informative sources
these things are ours as a matter of course

Learning the world is fraught with illusions
trials, injustice, and copious confusion

self-serving people, wealth, fame, and power
who enslave the innocent to build ivory towers

and what paths are there for us to choose
in a world we know is naught but a ruse

eternally seeking some hidden respite
becoming another deluded despot

thus all the things I had first believed
proved to be illusions and sadly naive

so instead of chasing a lost fantasy
or being pushed e'er harder toward apathy

and weary of enduring the status quo
political greed and assembly line woes

Jake Seveneau

All of this world's obvious ill-logic
its endless rules, wars, and projects

While residing in a nation that many call "Free"
that dresses dark secrets in panoplies

which recognizing is too much to bear
and trying as I might can no longer care

and worked very hard not to participate
just hold my tongue and slip out the gate

but discovering there's no place to live alone
beyond the cold grasp of all human thrones

Now I am pressed to ask the ultimate question
concerning this madness in infinite session

Should I check out early by my own hand
What would result from such a plan

Is suicide that simple and truly painless
or is such an idea sadly just gain-less

Would one enter a realm which is even worse
than this insane one I call by a curse

Making the logical option to suffer on
through all the crap this world spawns

gleaning what little good it might offer
placing such wisdom in a spiritual coffer

Is this meagre life worth the time
will it ever produce more than a few lousy rhymes

So far life has been one chaotic circus
and I really don't see the profit or purpose

So if you can, please answer this question
is suicide just a weakling's obsession

Is it better to drink a poisonous potion
and be found guilty of heinous notions

conspiracy for taking part in war
denying the truth and barring the door

claiming exception for some paltry reason
that seemed adequate in previous seasons

And still I must press the ultimate question
concerning this madness in infinite session

Should I check out early by my own hand
What would be the result of such a plan

36. Random Patterns

Random patterns plague my dreams
never the same these twisted schemes
yet all focus on familiar themes

war and hate, chaos and fear
it is all so dark and all too clear
screams and shouts I always hear

When will it ever end or can anyone say
tonight, tomorrow, another day
can anything make it go away

Random patterns with jagged edges
nightmare soup from Dante's dredges
where help is promised like political pledges

37. All in My Head

No sleep at all for days on end
Or else I sleep all day and night

in hyper-drive
or else dead stop

One or the other
no in between

dozens of migrating frequencies
varying volumes and clarity

each recognizable given time
but only sometimes comprehensible

Thoughts falling like pick-up-sticks
without rhythm, rhyme, or reason
lest it be intentional chaos

Random stimuli, flickering and flashing
twisting relationships, scenes and plots

Composed, played out and collated
by conflicted personalities

Jake Seveneau

one side depressed
the other manic

They say that it is all in my head
and clearly they are right
but I wish it was not

I wish it would stop and let me rest
seven to eight hours a day
every day
at least for a while

All in My Head

38. Bad Days

high volume
high speed
crowds like cattle milling

racing thoughts
too much input
too much pressure

flashbacks
flash-forwards

acceleration
anxiety
panic
pills

lack of prayer and meditation
crashing, burning
crawling under the bed
crying out
Oh God, please help me

Good Days

clarity
simplicity
prayer and meditation

gentle music
reading
writing
progressing education

giving, receiving
forgiveness
peace and harmony

touching souls
with truth and love
setting spirits free

Bad Days/Good Days

39. The Second War

They author
interpret
adjudicate the rules

So that all play along accordingly
Simon Says time and again

To heck with the truth
memorize the standard
present a textbook case
to their shrinks

Forget about logic
reality
meaning
purpose

recite the "truth" they ask you for

Like Alice through the looking glass
take your pills
recite the numbers
and then maybe we will send you home
at ten percent

Better luck next time

40. The Cure

The only cure for what ails us is prevention

to end all wars
end all anger and hate
all prejudice
conflicts

or perhaps in the end to just end it all

It may take a hundred generations
just to get started

Even then the only real cure is in us
to love our neighbour as ourselves

true freedom equals total forgiveness

Makes sense, does it not
Lord I hope I am right

Otherwise the only cure is to end it all

41. War and Peace

War!
Constantly declared
waged in various ways
      in all directions
always for the same reasons

Our refusal to see
we are all the same
      all prejudiced
      all egotistical
      all self-absorbed
 all in desperate need of repentance
                            forgiveness

Peace!
Sometimes dreamed of
occasionally attempted in small circles
                  in limited ways
always failing for the same reasons

Our refusal to admit
we are all the same
      all guilty
      all unreformed
      all in need of love

42. Shrink-Wrapped Sessions

Manic is frantic
depression regression
labels and pills
shrink-wrapped sessions

Packaged and priced
for the local bazaar
by the shakers and bakers
of the PDR

43. All I Can Do

Into the little town I wander
heart and soul in pocket
well secured
aiming for the Black and White Café

Like all such ideas this one began
with some degree of trepidation
although just once a week was proposed
for a while

after a half dozen visits
time sped up again
to twice a week

A mind as confused as mine
does not find comfort in busy places

Once upon a time
I loved cafes
coffeehouses
but not so much any more

Honestly
now I prefer
being alone at night
when the house is silent

Jake Seveneau

when others are sleeping
or during the day
when others are at work

44. To Be Healed

In this life there are but two things
I am concerned about

To begin with
I want to be healed
          physically
          mentally
             spiritually healed

I want to walk upright
      think upright
        be upright

Thus I pray daily
          hourly

that will be my nature

45. Total and Permanent

One Hundred Percent
Total and Permanent

labels of finality
fatality
fragility
living corpses more than less

Is it better than out on the streets

All we really want is to be needed
to forgive and be forgiven

to contribute
create and share
discuss the issues
work things out

to think a while
meditate
listen
talk

Instead we are held captive
examined
assessed

classified
labelled

dated
warehoused in some data bank

forgotten about
slowly covered in layers of dust
in preparation for carbon dating

Lab rats for the VA medical system

Is it better than out on the streets

46. Note to Self

The past will always exist
it cannot be erased
    cannot be altered
but
the present might be

Change environments
change habits
do not remain what you were
be better
love more

Choose to believe there is forgiveness
want it
ask for it
pray for it

Still the past will exist
but it should not affect the present as much

Consider that it is rainy, cool and peaceful here
though war continues in other locations

Bombs fall
rockets penetrate people's homes
children are killed

others become soldiers of vengeance and die slowly
from hate and confusion
    guilt and clarity

So how can I look away
        pretend it is not happening

Honestly I do not know
and yet I try
but for the sake of sanity

47. Saigon Has Fallen - 30 April 1975

Geographically far from Vietnam
in the mountains surrounding Hatcher's Pass
HAMs, Short waves, SSB and CBs
all report Saigon has fallen

Nearly three years since my reprieve
still my mind and soul are prisoners

A conch attempting to evade the draft
volunteering to act as a medic

a witness to many who paid the price

If there is anyone who has the answers
I would very much like to meet them

What was it actually all about
furthering confusion?

What did we learn, if anything,
that peace and love are fantasies

Has anyone actually benefitted
the Sultans of Sea-land and Khaki Mafia

Will healing and peace ever come

48. Last Will and Testimony

When my time comes I implore you
please do not leave me to the vultures of death
with their morbid sales pitches
supposedly selling dignity and honour
        peace and rest
             and other things
they know nothing about
those peddlers of lies

As the Lord is willing to let me rest
where and how my life dictates
first pray about what God has decided
not where and how they price a "good deal"

And do not let the serpent dance
no conga line of automobiles
no pennants fluttering briskly in the wind

Do not post my name and some old photo
with a miniscule biography
no names or stats
no one really cares about

And do not cover my coffin with the banner
of any state or nation

nor lay on me the symbol of any religious sect
to measure whether or not I am worthy of heaven

My prayers and confessions
    faith and works
are not the business of anyone
save our Father in Heaven

So do not waste a thought or breadth on me
when I depart

simply place my old tent on the fire
    or in the ground
and bequest my ashes unto the wind and rain
        seasons and soil
        creatures of earth
for my soul already belongs to God
and there is nothing you can do for me

And if you wish somehow to honor me
go to some mountain or valley
    desert or forest
    river or sea

and think of your own souls
of the fact you too belong to God
and one day will depart this physical realm

Then too seek truth
    race and faith
create beautiful things
serve and witness through your spiritual gifts

do good works

and above all else

love and care for each other

This is my last will and testimony

49. Postscript: **The Result**

There were a few decades bound up with PTSD
                un-diagnosed bipolar 2
                self-medication
                rarely attending church
                      reading the word

Often lodging at the Helping Hand Mission
        or an old van
        or on friends' couches

when I was refusing to go to any branch
of the government
                for any reason

Until I gave in
at my love's insistence
and returned to the Lord
     eventually found help
             was awarded a disability pension
which keeps me off the streets

Now
again I belong to Yeshua
      have long since forgiven any and all involved
           been forgiven by the Lord Jesus Christ

and this is the result
just a small book

An outsider's attempt to quietly communicate
with the world at large
penultimate warnings
penultimate blessings

Old Man